W9-BHG-507

We Love Spring!
RAINY DAY FUN

By Melba Dewberry

Gareth Stevens
PUBLISHING

Please visit our website, www.garethstevens.com. For a free color catalog of all our
high-quality books, call toll free 1-800-542-2595 or fax 1-877-542-2596.

Cataloging-in-Publication Data
Names: Dewberry, Melba.
Title: Rainy day fun / Melba Dewberry.
Description: New York : Gareth Stevens Publishing, 2017. | Series: We love spring! | Includes index.
Identifiers: ISBN 9781482455038 (pbk.) | ISBN 9781482455069 (library bound) | ISBN 9781482455052 (6 pack)
Subjects: LCSH: Rain and rainfall–Juvenile literature.
Classification: LCC QC924.7 D45 2017 | DDC 551.57'7–dc23

First Edition

Published in 2017 by
Gareth Stevens Publishing
111 East 14th Street, Suite 349
New York, NY 10003

Copyright © 2017 Gareth Stevens Publishing

Editor: Ryan Nagelhout
Designer: Samantha DeMartin

Photo credits: Cover, p. 1 Zoia Kostina/Shutterstock.com; p. 5 FamVeld/Shutterstock.com; p. 7 Lorena
Fernandez/Shutterstock.com; p. 9 Monkey Business Images/Shutterstock.com; pp. 11, 21 wavebreakmedia/
Shutterstock.com; p. 13 Gelpi/Shutterstock.com; p. 15 Sergey Novikov/Shutterstock.com; p. 17 Phase4Studios/
Shutterstock.com; p. 19 Pressmaster/Shutterstock.com; p. 21 oliveromg/Shutterstock.com; p. 23 iofoto/
Shutterstock.com; p. 24 (crayons) bogdan ionescu/Shutterstock.com; p. 24 (cookies) Kat Snowden/
Shutterstock.com; p. 24 (popcorn) Lisovskaya Natalia/Shutterstock.com.

Printed in the United States of America

CPSIA compliance information: Batch #CW17GS: For further information contact Gareth Stevens, New York, New York at 1-800-542-2595.

Contents

It is raining outside.

5

But you can have fun
in the house!

You can play games.

You can watch a movie.

You can make
some popcorn.

13

You can play dress-up!

You can make art!
You can draw with crayons.

You can tell a story.

You can help Dad make lunch.

You can help make cookies, too!

Words to Know

cookies

crayons

popcorn

Index

24